D1174289

BASILOSAURUS

J 569 ZABLU
Zabludoff, Marc.
Basilosaurus

OCT 2 1 '09

PREHISTORIC BEASTS
BASILOSAURUS

MARC ZABLUDOFF

ILLUSTRATED BY PETER BOLLINGER

Marshall Cavendish
Benchmark

New York

BURBANK PUBLIC LIBRARY

Marshall Cavendish Benchmark
99 White Plains Road
Tarrytown, NY 10591
www.marshallcavendish.us

Copyright © 2010 by Marshall Cavendish Corporation
All rights reserved.

No part of this book may be reproduced in any form without the written permission of the publisher.

All Internet addresses were correct and accurate at the time of printing.

Library of Congress Cataloging-in-Publication Data

Zabludoff, Marc.
Basilosaurus / by Marc Zabludoff ; illustrated by Peter Bollinger.
p. cm. — (Prehistoric beasts)
Includes bibliographical references and index.
Summary: "This series explores prehistoric beasts that roamed Earth and
its seas and each animal's physical characteristics, when and where each
animal lived, how they lived, what other animals lived alongside them, and
how we know this"—Provided by publisher.
ISBN 978-0-7614-3999-8
1. Basilosaurus—Juvenile literature. I. Bollinger, Peter. II. Title.
QE882.C5Z33 2010
569'.5—dc22
2008019723

Editor: Christine Florie
Publisher: Michelle Bisson
Art Director: Anahid Hamparian
Series Designer: Alicia Mikles

Photo research by Connie Gardner

The photographs in this book are used by permission and through the courtesy of:
Minden Pictures: Flip Nicklin, 10; Konrad Wothe, 14; *Getty Images:* Cris Bourooncle, 17.

Printed in Malaysia
1 3 5 6 4 2

CONTENTS

THE ARRIVAL OF A KING

Another bright, warm day, and the sunlight sparkles off the ripples on the surface of the sea. The water, as always, is warm. It practically hums with the busy motion of life. Fish of all sizes and colors glisten as they dart about, their bodies and tails vibrating from side to side. They travel in schools so thick, they seem to make the water solid. Occasionally a turtle swoops by, its legs pulling it gracefully through its watery world.

A few hundred yards away, on the shore, a small group of wolf-size, furry animals are searching for food. They are pawing through the thicket of mangrove trees that grow right down to the water. Unlike the fish, they are unaware of the giant that is now gliding through the water, just below the surface. The first thing to appear is its mouth. It is open slightly, revealing an impressive lineup of large, pointed teeth. Behind it comes a sleek body that seems to go on forever. Its long, long tail waves up and down like a

Basilosaurus **needed a large amount of food every day to fuel its huge body. Here it preys on small mammals along a shore.**

whip, snapping the wide tips that spread out like fins at its end.

The giant's strong front flippers pull it upward until its head rises above the water. Suddenly a blast of air forced through its nostrils announces its presence so loudly that even the furry animals on shore look up. In its way the sound is as grand as a fanfare of trumpets announcing the arrival of a king—an ancient king that goes by the name *Basilosaurus*.

A LONG TALE OF A WHALE

Basilosaurus was a fairly new resident of the seas 40 million years ago. It was also the biggest resident, stretching 60 feet end to end. At the time, this mighty hunter was the largest animal on Earth and the world's most fearsome **predator**. There was probably nothing in the sea that could threaten it. Sharks were among its favorite foods. Its mouth was filled with forty-two huge teeth. Up front they were pointed and cone-shaped, perfect for stabbing and grabbing **prey**. Further back were big, blocky teeth topped with ridges like steak knives, used for slicing up food.

Although it lived its whole life in the water, *Basilosaurus* was not a fish. Nor was it a reptile, like the ocean giants that had lived alongside the dinosaurs 25 million years earlier. *Basilosaurus* was a whale, which means it was an air-breathing mammal.

The mouth of *Basilosaurus* held forty-two razor-sharp teeth.

9

Like the whales of today, *Basilosaurus* had two flat **flukes** at the end of its long, powerful tail. Beating them up and down, it powered itself through the water. But in many other ways *Basilosaurus* was different from modern whales. For a creature its size it had an unusually small head, no more than 5 feet long. Today, a whale *Basilosaurus*'s size would have a head three or four times as big. It would have a much bigger brain, too.

Compared with the great hulks we are used to seeing, this ancient whale had a very slender body. Also unlike whales today, *Basilosaurus* had no blowhole on the top of its head. Rather, it had two nostrils toward

What are the similarities and differences between a modern whale and *Basilosaurus*?

the end of its long snout, very much like an animal that lived on land. To breathe, *Basilosaurus* had to lift its nose out of the water.

Finally, sticking out from the sides at the front of its body were flippers with elbows that could bend like a seal's. At the back were two tiny legs, just 18 inches or so long. At the ends of these legs were tiny feet and several tiny toes.

Basilosaurus's **back limbs were very small, considering the huge size of its body. They also had tiny toes!**

THE WRONG NAME?

Basilosaurus is an odd name for a whale. The *saurus* part means "lizard" or "reptile." *Basilo* is an ancient Greek word for "king." So how did a whale—a mammal—become "king of the reptiles?" Scientists discovered the beast in the 1830s, when a hill collapsed in Louisiana and revealed a long, curving backbone. Dr. Richard Harlan, the first to examine it, thought it came from a giant reptile, a 100-foot-long "sea serpent." So he gave the animal a name he thought was fitting. Other scientists soon realized the mistake, but it was too late. One of the rules scientists must follow is that the first name given to a **species** is the one it keeps—no matter how ill fitting it turns out to be.

WALK LIKE A WHALE

All members of the whale family, which includes whales, dolphins, and porpoises, are mammals. That means they breathe air, they give birth to live babies rather than laying eggs, and feed those babies with milk.

Many millions of years ago, though, all mammals started out as four-legged, land-dwelling animals covered with hair or fur. How do whales fit into that history?

Mammals first appeared on Earth when the dinosaurs were still ruling the planet. For a long time most mammals were shy, rat-size creatures living on seeds and insects. But after the dinosaurs went **extinct** 65 million years ago, mammals began to grow bigger and bolder. Within 10 million years, many mammals were at least wolf-size, and some were as large as cows.

Among them was a group of mammals called the **ungulates**. Ungulates are mammals that have toes protected by hooves, rather than nails or claws. Some ungulates have an odd number of toes on each foot, and some have an even number of toes.

The even-toed ungulates are called **artiodactyls**. Today, this group includes pigs, cows, sheep, goats, camels, and hippos. The animals that were the whale's ancestors were also artiodactyls. They had hooves and were used to walking and running on land. But around 54 million years ago, some of them started spending more time in the water.

More than 50 million years ago, some mammals, such as _Pakicetus_, began to prefer life in the water to life on dry land.

CONFUSING FAMILIES

The whale's ancestors were not the only mammals to head for the sea. Around the same time, the plant-eating ancestors of sea cows—manatees and dugongs—also took to the water. But sea cows and whales are not closely related. The whale's closest living relative is probably the hippopotamus. Sea cows are much more closely related to elephants.

Why would any mammals leave the land they were well adapted for? Because the seas offered them great opportunities. The oceans were filled with food— uncountable millions of fish, squid, turtles, and other animals. The oceans also held few competitors. True, there were some toothy sharks prowling the waters. But the really fierce predators—the great sea-dwelling reptiles known as **mosasaurs** and **plesiosaurs**—had all died out at the same time as the dinosaurs.

Gradually, over hundreds of thousands of years, the

This illustration shows the gradual evolution of some mammals as they evolved into sea-dwelling creatures.

Pakicetus

Rodhocetus

Ambulocetus

Protocetus

Basilosaurus

mammals' bodies began to **evolve**, or change. The bones of their separate "fingers" became joined by skin and turned into flippers. Their tails grew thicker and longer. They lost their fur, and their ears began to shrink.

Slowly, these land dwellers became sea dwellers. The first whales were probably something like a mix of a crocodile and a sea lion. They still had four legs that could hold them up on land and heavily webbed feet. But over time, as the front legs became powerful paddles, the rear legs got smaller and smaller. By the time *Basilosaurus* appeared, those rear legs were just 1.5 feet long—a size fit for a human toddler, not a 60-foot-long whale.

IF WHALES ARE MAMMALS, WHY DO THEY SWIM LIKE FISH?

Well, actually, they do not swim like fish. All fish move their bodies side to side. Whales and dolphins beat their tails up and down. That movement is a holdover from their past. On land, mammals developed spines that moved up and down when they galloped on their four legs. When the mammals that eventually became whales started to live in the water instead of on land, they used the up-and-down motion of their spines for swimming rather than running.

A WARMER WORLD

Basilosaurus was at home around the globe. Its **fossil** bones have been found from North America to Europe to North Africa, and it may have traveled as far as Australia. To be precise, a *Basilosaurus* fossil found in North America is not quite the same animal as, say, a *Basilosaurus* found in Egypt. The two belonged to different *Basilosaurus* species. But the difference between them was as small as, say, the difference between Asian elephants and African elephants. (African elephants are bigger than their Asian cousins and have bigger ears.)

All the *Basilosaurus* fossil sites are on dry

These *Basilosaurus* bones were found in the desert sands of Egypt, once an ancient sea.

land now, but millions of years ago they were at the bottoms of shallow seas. In fact, some of the best *Basilosaurus* fossil spots are in Egypt, in the middle of what is now a dry, sand dune—filled desert. This desert is where the first fossil leg bones of *Basilosaurus* were found, in 1989.

TOOTH PROOF

Basilosaurus was the first fossil animal to prove that the ancestors of whales were land-dwelling mammals. But the first proof of this was not the ancient whale's tiny rear legs. The first proof came from *Basilosaurus*'s teeth. When they were found in Alabama in the 1830s, scientists saw that *Basilosaurus* had different kinds of teeth—pointed biting teeth up front and grinding, slicing molars in back. Only mammals have teeth like this. Reptiles have teeth that are all the same.

When *Basilosaurus* was alive, this desert—and really, the whole planet—was a rather different place. Earth was warmer than it is now, and there were no great fields of ice at the North and South poles. In fact, there were forests near the poles, filled with plants that today grow only in the hot **tropics**.

Hard as it may be to imagine, our planet changes all the time, though the change happens too slowly for us to notice. In *Basilosaurus*'s time,

At different times, the changing seas have provided a comfortable home for a variety of fascinating animals.

40 million years ago, Earth's **continents** and oceans were arranged differently from how they are arranged now. North and South America were not joined, for example, and shallow, warm waters covered large parts of what is now Alabama, Louisiana, and Mississippi. These waters were home to generations of hungry, powerful whales.

Across the globe a long, shallow sea separated Africa from Europe and Asia. This long-vanished ocean, called the Tethys Sea, was a perfect hunting ground for *Basilosaurus*. It was warm, not too deep, and filled with fish and other animals.

Today, one end of the Tethys Sea is covered by the sands of the Egyptian desert. The sands are littered with thousands of ancient whale bones, and they give us some of the most dramatic evidence we have for how *Basilosaurus* lived.

DESERT TALES

Not all the bones in the Egyptian desert come from *Basilosaurus*. Many are from a different ancient whale called *Dorudon*. *Dorudon* was similar to *Basilosaurus* in many ways, though it was much smaller. *Dorudon* grew to be only 15 feet or so. But it, too, had a small head, tiny rear legs and feet, and a more flexible neck and flippers than today's whales—it could turn its head sideways and bend its flippers at the "elbows." It, too, was a fish-eating hunter.

Dorudon was another ancient whale that
lived during the time of ***Basilosaurus.***

The Egyptian fossils of *Basilosaurus* and *Dorudon* are found in the same spots. But there is an interesting difference between them. All the *Basilosaurus* bones are from adults. Many of the *Dorudon* bones, meanwhile, are from youngsters. Why such an odd combination of fossils?

Scientists think the fossil site was once a calm bay where every year, *Dorudon* females would come to have their babies. They would stay there, nursing the young whales until they were old enough to travel. *Basilosaurus* would come to this spot also. But it would come not to give birth, but to feed—on *Dorudon* youngsters.

There are whales today that follow this same strategy. Orcas, or killer whales, hunt in waters used as nurseries by humpback whales.

WAS BASILOSAURUS BIGGER THAN TODAY'S WHALES?

Basilosaurus was very long—at least 60 feet and perhaps a bit more—which means it was about the same size as today's sperm whales. Not many whales are longer, but there are a couple: Fin whales grow to be 88 feet long. Blue whales can reach a whopping 100 feet, which makes them not only bigger than *Basilosaurus* but also bigger than any other animal that has ever existed.

22

A ***Basilosaurus*** preys ➡
on a group of ***Dorudon***.

A VANISHING KINGDOM

Basilosaurus may indeed have been a king in its day. But as the world changed, it eventually had to give up its throne.

By 36 million years ago Earth was again becoming a different kind of planet. The shallow seas in which *Basilosaurus* swam were disappearing. Continents were on the move. Australia drifted farther away from Antarctica. Africa moved ever closer to Asia. The Tethys Sea was pinched closed. Earth began to grow much cooler. As the warm, shallow seas vanished, the fish and other sea life retreated to deeper water or disappeared.

Perhaps *Basilosaurus* was simply not built for this new world. It was not a deep diver—it could not hold its breath for very long. Perhaps it could not handle the colder temperatures. Or perhaps the other whales that appeared at this time were simply better swimmers and hunters.

◄ **Basilosaurus may have vanished as the warm seas shrank and the Earth's climate began to cool.**

Whatever the reason, over many thousands of years, *Basilosaurus* eventually died out. Its place was taken by new whale species much closer in design to the whales we know today.

Basilosaurus was probably not the direct ancestor of today's whales— it was not, for example, their great-great-great grandfather. Instead, it was more like their great-great-great grandfather's cousin. But it was an important member of the family—the first to achieve the giant size that has become so much a part of being a whale. It was also the first animal to give scientists proof that whales' ancestors once walked on land.

For that alone we should be grateful. *Basilosaurus* was a giant that pointed both to the past and to the future, showing us how life evolves on Earth in surprising and wonderful ways.

TIMELINE

500 million years ago	First fish appear in the sea.
380–375 million years ago	First four-legged animals appear.
340–310 million years ago	First reptiles appear.
230–225 million years ago	First dinosaurs and first mammals appear.
65 million years ago	Dinosaurs, mosasaurs, and plesiosaurs go extinct.
55–53 million years ago	Some mammals known as artiodactyls start spending more of their lives in the water.
53–50 million years ago	*Himalayacetus*, the oldest whale known, appears.
50–49 million years ago	*Ambulocetus*, a whale with sea lion–like legs, appears.
46 million years ago	Whales become fully adapted to life in the water.
40 million years ago	*Basilosaurus* and *Dorudon*, which actually swim like modern whales, appear.
36 million years ago	Earth begins to cool; *Basilosaurus* and *Dorudon* go extinct.
35 million years ago	Modern-looking whales, without legs, appear.

GLOSSARY

artiodactyls (ahr-tee-oh-DAK-tils) group of mammals that appeared around 65 million years ago; they have hooves and an even number of toes. Also called even-toed ungulates.

continents   the seven great bodies of land on Earth.

evolve   to change over time.

extinct   gone forever.

flukes   the two broad, flat parts at the end of the tail of a whale or dolphin.

fossil   the remains of an animal or plant that lived long ago.

mosasaur   (MOH-suh-sawr) extinct, long-jawed, sea-dwelling reptile that grew up to 30 feet long.

plesiosaur   (PLEE-see-uh-sawr) extinct, sea-dwelling reptile with needle-sharp teeth, paddle-shaped legs, and often a long neck.

predator   an animal that hunts and eats other animals.

prey   an animal that is hunted by a predator.

species   particular kinds of plants or animals, different from all others.

tropics   areas around the middle of the planet where it is nearly always hot.

ungulate   (UHNG-guh-lit) hoofed animals.

FIND OUT MORE

Books

Lessem, Don. *Sea Giants of Dinosaur Time*. Minneapolis, MN: Lerner Publications, 2005.

Marven, Nigel. *Chased by Sea Monsters*. New York: DK, 2004.

Web Sites

How Whales Work

http://science.howstuffworks.com/whale.htm

This site may be a bit advanced, but it is accessible if a parent is there to help. It is filled with tons of information about modern whales and dolphins.

Life in the Ancient Seas

http://www.mnh.si.edu/museum/VirtualTour/Tour/First/Seas/index.html

This site, from the Smithsonian Institution, gives a brief look at *Basilosaurus* and other extinct critters.

Life on the Bay

http://www.mbayaq.org/efc/mbay.asp

Go to this part of the Monterey Bay Aquarium's Web site for information about marine mammals and other life in the waters off California.

INDEX

Page numbers in **boldface** are illustrations.

ABOUT THE AUTHOR

Marc Zabludoff, the former editor in chief of *Discover* magazine, has been involved in communicating science to the public for more than two decades. His other work for Marshall Cavendish includes books on spiders, beetles, and monkeys in the AnimalWays series, along with books on insects, reptiles, and the largely unknown and chiefly microscopic organisms known as protoctists. Zabludoff lives in New York City with his wife and daughter.

ABOUT THE ILLUSTRATOR

Peter Bollinger is an award-winning illustrator whose clients include those in the publishing, advertising, and entertainment industries. Bollinger works in two separate styles, traditional airbrush and digital illustration. He lives in California with his wife, son, and daughter.